Short Stories in English for Intermediate Level ESL/EFL Learners:

Improve Reading Comprehension with Stories about Life in Canada

Jackie Bolen

www.eslspeaking.org

D1732279

Table of Contents

About the Author: Jackie Bolen

I taught English in South Korea for 10 years to every level and type of student. I've taught every age from kindergarten kids to adults. Most of my time has centered around teaching at two universities: five years at a science and engineering school in Cheonan, and four years at a major university in Busan where I taught upper-level classes for students majoring in English. In my spare time, you can usually find me outside surfing, biking, hiking, or snowshoeing. I now live in Vancouver, Canada.

In case you were wondering what my academic qualifications are, I hold a Master of Arts in Psychology. During my time in Korea, I completed both the Cambridge CELTA and DELTA certification programs. With the combination of almost ten years teaching ESL/EFL learners of all ages and levels, and the more formal teaching qualifications I've obtained, I have a solid foundation on which to offer advice to English learners.

Please send me an email with any questions or feedback that you might have.

YouTube: www.youtube.com/c/jackiebolen

Pinterest: www.pinterest.com/eslspeaking

ESL Speaking: www.eslspeaking.org

Email: jb.business.online@gmail.com

You might also be interested in these books (by Jackie Bolen):

• Master English Collocations in 15 Minutes a Day

• IELTS Academic Vocabulary Builder

How to Use this Book

This book is ideal for people who want to improve their reading comprehension skills and vocabulary. Or for people who are preparing to move to Canada and want to learn a little bit about the culture before doing that.

To get the most bang for your buck, I recommend doing the following:

- Read one story a day, instead of all the stories in a single day! The best readers are those who do it consistently each day.

- Be sure to do the questions for each story.

- Pay attention to the vocabulary words in **bold** (letters that are darker). Try to guess the meaning of the word, considering the other words in the sentence before looking it up in a dictionary. After that, write down any words that you don't know in a notebook to review later. Also consider making flashcards for these new words.

- Read the stories with a friend if possible. Discuss the questions together.

- If you're using this book to improve your TOEFL, TOEIC or IELTS reading scores, be sure to read the questions first so you can scan for the answers instead of reading every single word. After doing this, take more time to read the story in full.

Min-Gyu is Going to Canada

Reading strategy focus: *Look at the questions (see below the story) first. Think about the key words in each question and what kind of information you'll need to find in the story.*

Min-Gyu is having trouble sleeping. He is going to be leaving Korea for the first time the next morning. Actually, that isn't 100% correct. He had gone to Japan when he was in high school with his classmates. But this would be his first time traveling alone. That's why he's so **nervous**.

Min-Gyu is flying to Vancouver at 1:30 pm. He will start English classes in a few days. Of course, he doesn't plan to only study. He wants to experience Canadian culture, visit Stanley Park, try Canadian food and maybe go skiing in Whistler. He'd love to see the Rocky Mountains too. And hopefully make some friends from other countries to practice his English with. Maybe even try online dating with some Canadians!

His parents and brother are going to take him to the airport in **a couple of hours**. Some of his close friends will be there too. He thinks he'll probably cry, which might be kind of embarrassing. He's twenty years old now, not a child. It will be difficult to say goodbye. He's known these friends his **entire life**, since elementary school.

Right now, he's checking to make sure he has everything he needs. Passport, phone charger, **power converter**, Korean snacks, laptop, and cord. A book for the plane. A sweater in case it's cold. He's ready to go. His **suitcase** is very heavy though because he has everything he needs for a year.

His mom says, "Min-Gyu. Do you have everything? Are you ready?" He answers, "Yes, mom. I've got everything." His mom responds, "Come have some lunch. I've made your favourite—kimchi **stew**." His family eats lunch together. Everyone is quiet and not talking that much. They're thinking about Min-Gyu leaving for one year and how much they'll miss each other.

6

After lunch, his family starts bringing his things to the car. His parents look sad. He feels very sad too but also excited about his new life in Canada. They drive to Incheon airport together, listening to pop songs on the radio. Min-Gyu looks out the window. So many **thoughts** are going around inside his head.

Finally, they arrive at the airport. Everyone is bustling around, getting his luggage out of the car, and taking pictures. He sees his friends who are already there. Min-Gyu gets his ticket at the check-in machine and drops off his luggage. It's time to go through immigration. He quickly hugs everyone goodbye and tries not to cry. He looks back one last time before he goes through the door and waves. He's ready to start his adventure in Canada.

Vocabulary

nervous: Worried or anxious feeling.

a couple of hours: Two hours.

entire life: From birth to the present time. For Min-Gyu, from 0-20 years (he's 20 years old now).

power converter: Something that allows you to use an electronic device in a different country, even if the plug shape/size is different.

suitcase: A kind of bag that people take on a trip or vacation. Square or rectangle shape.

stew: A kind of food. Like a soup but thicker.

thoughts: Ideas or opinions, inside your mind.

Comprehension Questions

1. Where is Min-Gyu going? Why?
2. Who is taking him to the airport?
3. Has he traveled alone before?
4. How does Min-Gyu feel today?
5. Why is his suitcase heavy?
6. Who does he want to practice English with?

Answers

1. He's going to Canada to study English.
2. His parents and brother are taking him to the airport.
3. No, he's never traveled alone.
4. He feels sad, excited, and nervous.
5. His suitcase is heavy because he has many things. He's going to Canada for one year.
6. He hopes to practice English with some friends from other countries.

Synonym Practice: Think of two other words or phrases that have the same meaning as the vocabulary words from the story. Do NOT look at the definitions again, if possible.

1. suitcase: _____, _____

2. nervous: _____, _____

3. thoughts: _____, _____

Summarize the Story

Using 1-2 sentences, summarize the story. Include only the main details and key events.

Summary:

New Words

Write down any new words that you learned from this story. Consider writing them in a vocabulary notebook or making some flashcards for further review.

-

-

-

Let's Talk More

Talk with a friend or classmate about these questions. If you're studying alone, write down 2-3 sentences for each question.

1. Have you ever been to another country by yourself? What was that experience like?

2. Would you like to study English in another country? Why or why not?

3. What do you think are some things that Min-Gyu will miss about Korea?

4. Have you ever felt really nervous about something you were going to do? What was it?

Who is That?

Reading strategy focus: *Scan the story quickly (set a timer for 30 seconds). Answer this question: Jay will meet the woman that he noticed (T/F). See answer below the story. Then, read the questions and read the story again, more slowly.*

Jay was at the movie theater with his two friends, Keith and Tony. They were going to watch the new Superman movie. It was popular and difficult to get tickets to. But his friend Keith **reserved** some online for them. He was good at doing stuff like that.

They had to wait in line at the theater to **pick up** their tickets. It was a Friday night, so it was quite busy. Just in front of them was a group of women around the same age as them. Jay noticed one of the women in front of him. She had long, beautiful hair and was wearing nice jeans and a sweater. "Who is that?," he thought to himself, "She is beautiful."

Jay was **lost in his own thoughts** about the woman in front of him and not listening to his friends. Keith and Tony laughed loudly at a joke, and the woman turned around to see who was laughing. She looked at all of them and then smiled at Jay. They made **eye contact,** and he smiled back. Jay wanted to talk to her, but he was nervous so he didn't.

They finally got their tickets and went to the **concession** to get some drinks and popcorn for the movie. Jay told his friends about this beautiful woman. They said that he should go say hi, but he knew that he never would! He was too **shy** to do that kind of thing. His friends said he was making a mistake and that he'd regret it.

They got their popcorn and drinks, and Tony grabbed a napkin. He asked someone who worked at the movie theater for a pen. Jay thought it was strange to be asking for a pen at the movie theater but didn't pay attention to him. Tony asked Jay to show him which woman he thought was beautiful. He pointed her out, sitting on a bench, waiting for the movie to start. Tony walked over and handed her the napkin.

Jay said, "TONY! What did you do?" Tony said, "I wrote down your name and phone number on the napkin and said that you wanted to go on a date with her. You're welcome! Hahahaha!"

Then, they had to go into the movie theater. They sat down, and Jay's phone **buzzed**. It was the woman, introducing herself. She said that they should go for a drink after the movie. Jay quickly said yes, and they made plans to meet at a pub that was very close to the movie theater. Jay was excited and could hardly concentrate on the movie! It seemed to go on forever.

Reading strategy focus answer: True

Vocabulary

reserved: Booked ahead of time. For example, tickets or a table at a restaurant.

pick up: Get something or someone from somewhere.

lost in his own thoughts: Thinking about something, not paying attention to other people; daydreaming.

eye contact: When two people look directly into each other's eyes.

concession: A place to buy snacks or drinks at a movie theater or sports event.

shy: Finds it difficult to talk to people, especially people they don't know well.

buzzed: Made a sound or vibration, usually refers to a cellphone when you get a message.

Comprehension Questions

1. Who got the tickets for them?
2. Who noticed the beautiful woman?
3. When did Jay first notice her?
4. How did Jay get her phone number?
5. Is Jay going to meet the woman?
6. Do you think that Tony is a good friend? Why?

Answers

1. Keith reserved the tickets.
2. Jay noticed the woman.
3. He noticed her when they were standing in line at the movie theater.
4. Tony gave Jay's phone number to the woman on a napkin.
5. Yes, Jay is going to meet the woman after the movie.
6. (many answers possible).

Synonym Practice: Think of two other words or phrases that have the same meaning as the vocabulary words from the story. Do NOT look at the definitions again, if possible.

1. pick up : _____, _____
2. concession: _____, _____
3. shy: _____, _____

Summarize the Story

Using 1-2 sentences, summarize the story. Include only the main details and key events.

Summary:

New Words

Write down any new words that you learned from this story. Consider writing them in a vocabulary notebook or making some flashcards for further review.

-
-
-

Let's Talk More

Talk with a friend or classmate about these questions. If you're studying alone, write down 2-3 sentences for each question. There is no correct answer—give your opinion!

1. Would you ever do something similar to what Tony did?
2. Have you met a boyfriend or girlfriend on a dating app? How about "in real life?"
3. What are some movie theater etiquette rules (how to be polite) in your country?
4. Do you prefer to watch movies at home or in a movie theater? Why?

Camping in Golden Ears

Reading Strategy Focus: *Read the title and first paragraph only. Make three predictions about what you think might happen in the story. Write them down. Read the story to see if any of your predictions are correct.*

Jenny had never been **camping** before. Her parents didn't like sleeping outside! But she thought it seemed fun and liked campfires. She was a bit nervous about bears and other animals when sleeping in a tent though.

Her friends, Carrie and Jill asked her to join them at Golden Ears, a beautiful park near Vancouver for three nights in July. It was difficult to get a **reservation,** but they were successful! She said yes and then asked Jill what she needed to bring.

Jill said that she had a big tent they could all share. But she needed to bring a camping mat because the ground was going to be hard, as well as a sleeping bag. Plus, lots of beer! Jill said that she could make **meals** for everyone and that Jenny could give her some money to pay for food. Maybe around $20 for the weekend.

The trip was coming up soon, so Jenny started to pack her things. Clothes, snacks, beer, and things for swimming and hiking. She asked Carrie **a million questions** about what to bring but Carrie was patient and answered them all.

Finally, the day was here! Jill and Carrie picked her up and they drove to Golden Ears Park. It was a beautiful drive and thankfully, it wasn't raining. It was **clear** and hot. They arrived at their campsite, opened up a beer and set up the tent and everything else they needed. It was **cozy**. Jenny was sure she'd have an enjoyable few days.

Jill wanted to go for a swim, but Carrie wanted to relax at the campsite and read a book. Jenny wanted to go swimming, so her and Jill walked to the lake. It took only a few minutes. They swam, but the water was so cold! It was refreshing though because it was such a hot day. They started to get hungry, so went back to the campsite to make dinner.

When it started to get dark, they made a fire and drank lots of beers and told scary stories. They saw many stars because it was so dark out. Finally, they started to get sleepy. Plus, they were running out of firewood. Jenny looked at her phone to see the time and was surprised to see it was already 3 am! They got into their sleeping bags and slept in until it started to get hot inside the tent. All in all, Jenny had a great time camping at Golden Ears and was thankful Jill and Carrie **invited** her.

Vocabulary

camping: Sleeping outside in a tent.

reservation: Saving something. In this case, a campsite for specific days.

meals: Breakfast, lunch or dinner.

a million questions: An expression that means many questions.

clear: Not cloudy.

cozy: Inviting; relaxing. A good atmosphere.

invited: Asked someone to join you for something.

Comprehension Questions

1. How many times had Jenny been camping?
2. How was the weather?
3. Who is cooking?
4. Who went swimming?
5. What did they do at night?
6. Did Jenny like camping?

Answers

1. She had never been camping.
2. It was great—hot and sunny. No rain.
3. Jill is cooking on this trip.
4. Jenny and Jill went swimming, but Carrie didn't.
5. They had a campfire, told stories, and drank beer.
6. Yes, she did.

Synonym Practice: Think of two other words that have the same meaning as the vocabulary words from the story. Do NOT look at the definitions again, if possible.

1. cozy: _____, _____
2. camping: _____, _____
3. clear: _____, _____

Summarize the Story

Using 1-2 sentences, summarize the story. Include only the main details and key events.

Summary:

New Words

Write down any new words that you learned from this story. Consider writing them in a vocabulary notebook or making some flashcards for further review.

-
-
-

Let's Talk More

Talk with a friend or classmate about these questions. If you're studying alone, write down 2-3 sentences for each question. There is no correct answer—give your opinion!

1. Have you ever been camping before? If yes, how was that experience? If no, would you like to go in the future?
2. Besides bears, what are some difficulties that people might have when they're camping?
3. Do you like trying things that you've never done before? Or, do you prefer doing the usual things?
4. List 10 things you have to pack when you go camping.

The New Italian Restaurant

Reading strategy focus: *Look at the words in* **bold**. *If you don't know the meaning, make a guess based on the other words in the sentence. Do not use a dictionary. Then, read the questions below and the story.*

Sam and Tony were out for a walk in their neighborhood when they noticed a big line up. "I wonder why they're lining up? Hmmm. It looks like a new restaurant," said Tony. They asked someone in the line what they were waiting for. The person said that it's a new Italian restaurant, Luigi's. They had become popular because of a **review** in the *Vancouver Sun*. The person reviewing the restaurant loved it and said that it was now the best Italian in Vancouver. This made everyone want to try it as well!

Sam and Tony decided to **check it out** on Friday night. Tony called to make a reservation, but Luigi's said that they don't take reservations. They would just have to line up and hopefully get a seat. Sam guessed that it wouldn't be that busy if they went earlier, so they decided to go at 5:00.

Friday night came, and they walked over to Luigi's. They got there at 5:00, and there was already a line up of about 20 people. They decided to wait. It would probably be worth it. Sam and Tony chatted with people while they waited. Everyone was excited to try the food. Some people were going to try the pasta while others wanted pizza. Luigi's used a brick oven for making pizza, just like in Italy.

Finally, after about an hour, they got a table. Sam ordered a glass of white wine while Tony went with red. The waiter also brought them some bread and oil and balsamic vinegar to dip it in. They ordered two things to share: spaghetti & meatballs and a **margherita pizza**. They liked to try a bit of everything, so they usually ordered things to share. The food came quickly, which surprised them because the restaurant was **packed.**

The wait was worth it. It was the best Italian food either of them had ever tried.

Although it was expensive, it was worth it. Lining up for an hour was also worth it! The food was so delicious. For dessert, they had homemade **tiramisu** and some Italian coffee. When the meal was done, they paid the bill and left a generous **tip**. Sam said, "Tomorrow night? Same time, same place?" He was joking, but Tony said, "YES! I want to try everything."

Vocabulary

review: An opinion about something. In this case, about Luigi's restaurant.

the Vancouver Sun: A newspaper in Vancouver.

check it out: Go to, look at, examine, etc. In this case, go to the restaurant.

margherita pizza: Pizza with tomato sauce, basil and mozzarella cheese.

packed: Filled with people; completely full.

tiramisu: An Italian dessert.

tip: Money someone gives for good service at a restaurant, hotel, hair shop, etc.

Comprehension Questions

1. Why is Luigi's so busy?
2. Does the restaurant take reservations?
3. When did they decide to go there?
4. Why did Sam and Tony go there at 5:00?
5. What did they order?
6. Did they like the food?

Answers

1. It's because of a good review in the *Vancouver Sun*.
2. They don't take reservations.
3. They decided to go on Friday for dinner.
4. They thought it wouldn't be so busy at 5:00 (instead of later).
5. They ordered wine, pizza, pasta, tiramisu and coffee.
6. They loved it. They want to go back soon!

Synonym Practice: Think of two other words or phrases that have the same meaning as the vocabulary words from the story. Do NOT look at the definitions again, if possible.

1. check out: _____, _____

2. packed: _____, _____

3. review: _____, _____

Summarize the Story

Using 1-2 sentences, summarize the story. Include only the main details and key events.

Summary:

New Words

Write down any new words that you learned from this story. Consider writing them in a vocabulary notebook or making some flashcards for further review.

-

-

-

Let's Talk More

Talk with a friend or classmate about these questions. If you're studying alone, write down 2-3 sentences for each question. There is no correct answer—give your opinion!

1. Have you ever waited in a long line at a restaurant? Was it worth it?

2. What's the best meal you've ever had at a restaurant? Was it a very expensive place?

3. Do you like Italian food? Why or why not?

4. What's your favourite kind of food to eat in a restaurant? Why?

The Blind Date

Reading strategy focus: *Scan the story quickly (set a timer for 30 seconds). Answer this question: Will Sandy and Lucy go on another date? (yes/no). See answer below the story. Then, read the questions and read the story again, more slowly.*

Sandy recently **broke up** with her girlfriend and was feeling sad. They had been together for five years. She was talking to her friends about it when they were having coffee at Starbucks. One of her friends, Sarah said, "Sandy! I know the perfect person for you. She is recently **single** too."

Sarah's friends laughed. She was happily married and always trying to set up her single friends. She was **famous for it.** However, she was successful sometimes so her friends often let her do it. Some people she had set up had even gotten married. Sandy said, "Who is it?"

Sarah told everyone about one of her co-workers, Lucy. She had just moved to Toronto recently and started working at Sarah's company. Sarah said that she was beautiful, athletic, and nice as well. Sandy was **uncertain**. She still felt sad about her previous girlfriend. But her friends said that she had nothing to lose and should meet Lucy. Sandy **reluctantly** agreed, and Sarah said that she'd talk to Lucy on Monday at work and see what she thought. Sandy felt nervous, even thinking about it.

On Monday afternoon, Sandy got a text from Sarah. Lucy agreed to meet her and would send a text tonight after work. After work, Sandy got a text message from Lucy that said, "Hi! I'm Lucy. Nice to meet you. I've heard a lot about you. Would you like to meet up this week for a walk?" Sandy agreed, and they made a plan to meet on Wednesday. Sandy felt nervous but also excited. Lucy seemed amazing, according to Sarah.

On Wednesday, they met at a local park. Lucy was beautiful and engaging, just like Sarah promised. Sandy had a great time, and it was easy to talk to Lucy. After the date,

Sandy went home and then sent Lucy a text. She said, "It was nice to meet you. Would you like to meet up this weekend?" Lucy replied, "It was nice to meet you, too. But **you're not my type**. Maybe we could be friends." It wasn't the answer that Sandy expected.

Reading strategy focus answer: No.

Vocabulary

blind date: Going on a date with someone that you've never met in real life.

broke up: Ended a romantic relationship (marriage, or boyfriend/girlfriend).

single: No husband/wife/boyfriend/girlfriend.

famous for it: Known for doing something a lot.

uncertain: Not sure.

reluctantly: With hesitation.

you're not my type: You're not the kind of person I usually like in a romantic way.

Comprehension Questions

1. Why is Sandy feeling sad?
2. What is Sarah famous for?
3. Is Sarah married?
4. When and where did Sandy and Lucy meet?
5. What did Sandy think about Lucy?
6. What did Lucy think about Sandy?

Answers

1. Sandy ended her relationship a little while ago and is feeling depressed about it.
2. She is famous for setting up her single friends.
3. Yes, she is happily married.
4. They met on Wednesday at a park.
5. She thought Lucy was beautiful and engaging.
6. Lucy thought that Sandy wasn't her type.

Synonym Practice: Think of two other words or phrases that have the same meaning as the vocabulary words from the story. Do NOT look at the definitions again, if possible.

1. broke up: _____, _____

2. uncertain: _____, _____

3. reluctantly: _____, _____

Summarize the Story

Using 1-2 sentences, summarize the story. Include only the main details and key events.
Summary:

New Words

Write down any new words that you learned from this story. Consider writing them in a vocabulary notebook or making some flashcards for further review.

-

-

-

Let's Talk More

Talk with a friend or classmate about these questions. If you're studying alone, write down 2-3 sentences for each question. There is no correct answer—give your opinion!

1. Have you ever been on a blind date? How did it go?

2. Have you ever set someone up on a date? How did it go?

3. What's the best way to meet a boyfriend or girlfriend where you live?

4. What are some of the positive and negative things about being single?

Kiyo Goes Canoeing

Reading Strategy Focus: *Look at the questions (see below the story) first. Think about the key words in each question and what kind of information you'll need to find in the story.*

Kiyo had just moved to Canada a couple of years ago for university. She was studying at the University of Alberta, in Edmonton. Edmonton is famous for two things—how cold it is in winter and also that it has one of the biggest shopping malls in the world. However, the summers are beautiful. Edmonton is quite far north, so the summer days are very long. The **sun rises** at 5 am, and the **sun sets** after 10 pm. It's perfect if you like doing outdoor activities like boating, hiking, or cycling.

One of Kiyo's friends, Cindy, loves canoeing. She liked to go on the lakes and rivers around Edmonton almost every weekend during the summer. Kiyo always looked at the pictures on *Facebook* and commented about how fun it looked. She had never been canoeing before. It wasn't popular in Japan, where she came from.

One day, Cindy asked Kiyo if she was busy that weekend. She wanted to do an overnight canoe trip on the North Saskatchewan River, one of the longest rivers in Western Canada and wanted Kiyo to come with her. Kiyo immediately said yes but asked if Cindy was sure about taking her on an overnight trip for her first time. Cindy told her not to worry. She'd prepare everything, and it'd be fun. And Cindy's brother would **drop them off** at the starting point and then **pick them up** at the ending point the next day. It would be easy paddling because of the moving river.

Finally, it was time to start their trip. The **weather forecast** showed rain all weekend. When Kiyo asked Cindy about it, she said it was fine and told her to bring a rain jacket and some extra clothes. She went canoeing in the rain all the time. Kiyo reluctantly agreed and packed extra things. But she was actually quite worried about the weather.

Cindy's brother picked Kiyo up. The canoe was already on the roof of the **van**. It was raining heavily. They drove to the start point and unloaded everything from the van into the canoe. Kiyo was already **soaking wet** but didn't complain! They paddled for hours and as they were stopping for the night, the sun came out. "Thank god," Kiyo thought to herself. She felt so cold and grumpy!

Vocabulary

sun rises: When the sun comes up in the morning.

sun sets: When the sun goes down at night.

drop them off: Leave people somewhere.

pick them up: Get people from somewhere.

weather forecast: Prediction about the weather. Rainy, sunny, cloudy, etc.

van: A vehicle that's larger than a car. Usually a rectangle shape.

soaking wet: Very wet.

Comprehension Questions

1. Why is Kiyo in Edmonton?
2. What is Edmonton famous for?
3. How many hours of sunlight is there in the summer?
4. Why had Kiyo never been canoeing?
5. What did Kiyo have to bring?
6. Why was Kiyo happy at the end?

Answers

1. She's a student at the University of Alberta (UofA), located in Edmonton.
2. It's famous for a big mall and being cold in the winter. However, the summers are beautiful.
3. There's 17 hours of sunlight a day in the summer.
4. She'd never been canoeing because it's not popular in Japan.
5. She had to bring clothes and a rain jacket.
6. She was happy at the end because the rain stopped and the sun came out.

Synonym Practice: Think of two other words or phrases that have the same meaning as the

vocabulary words from the story. Do NOT look at the definitions again, if possible.

1. pick up: _____, _____
2. soaking wet: _____, _____
3. drop off: _____, _____

Summarize the Story

Using 1-2 sentences, summarize the story. Include only the main details and key events.

Summary:

New Words

Write down any new words that you learned from this story. Consider writing them in a vocabulary notebook or making some flashcards for further review.

-

-

-

Let's Talk More

Talk with a friend or classmate about these questions. If you're studying alone, write down 2-3 sentences for each question. There is no correct answer—give your opinion!

1. Is the place where you live famous for anything?
2. If you were Kiyo and saw that it was going to be rainy all weekend, would you have gone canoeing or cancelled?
3. Have you ever done something outside like hiking or camping when it's been really rainy?
4. What are some things that people visiting your country should try?

A Summer BBQ

Reading strategy focus: *Look at the words in **bold***. *If you don't know the meaning, make a guess based on the other words in the sentence. Do not use a dictionary. Then, read the questions below and the story.*

Summertime in Canada's capital city, Ottawa is beautiful. The days are long and the weather is hot and sunny. People that have houses with **backyards** love to have summer BBQs with family and friends. People without yards often take a portable BBQ to the park. It was one of Ted's favourite things to do in the summer.

Ted decided to have a BBQ for his birthday on June 3rd. It was a Saturday which was perfect because most people would be free. He invited all of his coworkers since he worked with only a few people. He also invited some neighbors that he liked and a few friends. Plus, his sister and her family too. Most people said that they could come so there would be about 25 in total. He was happy that most people agreed to come.

He asked everyone to bring a chair to sit on, some drinks and a side dish like potato chips, watermelon or salad. He planned to BBQ some chicken for the **meat eaters** and some tofu for the **vegans**. Ted bought lots of beer and made a big potato salad as well. He also bought some paper plates and cups, as well as **utensils** because he didn't want to wash dishes for 25 people! He didn't even have enough normal plates, cups and metal utensils for so many people.

On the morning of the party, he took out all of his outdoor chairs and BBQ from the garage. He got his biggest **cooler** and filled it with ice and beer. He **marinated** the chicken and tofu in some homemade BBQ sauce and put it back in the fridge. Plus, he cleaned the bathroom. All that was left was for the guests to arrive. He felt a little bit nervous because he hoped that everyone would have a fun time. But, he was also excited to see everyone and have some fun!

The guests began to arrive at 3:00, bringing lots of delicious food and drinks with them. Almost everyone knew each other already and they were having a great time. There was lots of conversation and laughing.

Once everyone was there, Ted turned on the BBQ and began cooking the chicken and tofu. The BBQ was a little bit hot and he was worried about the chicken burning but not being cooked on the inside, so he turned it down. Finally, it was done, and everyone grabbed a piece. The party was quiet as everyone was eating. It must have been delicious!

Vocabulary

summertime: Summer. In Canada, the months of June-August.

backyard: A place with grass behind a house.

meat eaters: People who eat meat like beef, pork, or chicken.

vegans: People who don't eat animal products.

utensils: Spoons, forks and knives.

cooler: A box to put ice and food/drinks in to keep things cold.

marinate: Put something like meat or tofu in sauce or spices before cooking for a few hours.

Comprehension Questions

1. Where do people like to BBQ in Ottawa?
2. What is Ted going to do for his birthday?
3. What did people have to bring to the party?
4. How many people are coming?
5. What did Ted make for the party?
6. Did everyone like the food?

Answers

1. People with big backyards like to BBQ there. However, people with very small or no backyards like to BBQ in public places like a park.
2. He is going to have a BBQ at his house.
3. They have to bring a chair, drinks and a side dish.
4. Around 25 people are coming to the party.
5. He made chicken, tofu and potato salad.
6. They probably liked it. Everyone was eating, and not talking.

Synonym Practice: Think of two other words or phrases that have the same meaning as the

vocabulary words from the story. Do NOT look at the definitions again, if possible.

1. meat eaters: _____, _____
2. utensils: _____, _____
3. cooler: _____, _____

Summarize the Story

Using 1-2 sentences, summarize the story. Include only the main details and key events.

Summary:

New Words

Write down any new words that you learned from this story. Consider writing them in a vocabulary notebook or making some flashcards for further review.

-

-

-

Let's Talk More

Talk with a friend or classmate about these questions. If you're studying alone, write down 2-3 sentences for each question. There is no correct answer—give your opinion!

1. Have you ever been to a backyard BBQ party? What did you think about it?
2. Do you think that Ted prepared well for the party? Why or why not?
3. What are some things that make a good party? Have you ever been to a terrible party? What went wrong?
4. Do you enjoy cooking and eating outside? Why or why not?

Watching Hockey

Reading strategy focus: *Scan the story quickly (set a timer for 30 seconds). Answer this question: Is Lucy happy or sad about the outcome of the game? See answer below the story. Then, read the questions and read the story again, more slowly.*

Lucy had loved watching hockey for as long as she could remember. She grew up in Edmonton during the 1980's and watched some of the most famous players there: Wayne Gretzky, Paul Coffee, Yari Kurri, Mark Messier, and others. One of her favourite memories was watching Edmonton win the **Stanley Cup** many times when she was young. Her dad used to take her to the games when she was little.

Hockey is probably the most popular sport in Canada. It makes sense. Canada is a big place with cold winters and lots of snow and ice! Many boys and girls play hockey when they're kids. Some of them will even play in the Olympics or the **NHL**. People that like hockey usually have a favourite team that they cheer for. The Toronto Maple Leafs and the Vancouver Canucks are the most popular teams in Canada. However, Edmonton now has the best player in the world, Connor McDavid, so they're becoming more popular.

Lucy now lives in Calgary, but her favourite team is still the Edmonton Oilers. The Calgary Flames and Edmonton Oilers are in the same province, Alberta. When they play each other, it's called, "The Battle of Alberta." The teams and the fans don't like each other very much, and there are often fights among players.

The Oilers were coming to play in Calgary so Lucy and her friend (also a fan of the Oilers) got tickets. They wore their Oilers **jerseys** and hats to the game and **cheered** loudly whenever the Oilers made a good play or got a goal. Everyone around them was angry and annoyed at them for cheering for Edmonton, instead of Calgary. But Lucy and her friend just laughed and cheered louder. There were only a few Edmonton fans in the whole arena.

There are three, 20-minute periods in a hockey game. The Flames were leading 2-0 after the end of the first period. The two teams played the second period, and it was still 2-0. In the third period, the Oilers scored two goals in the first few minutes. The game was **tied.** When there was only 3 minutes left, the Oiler's captain, Connor McDavid scored a beautiful **goal**. In the end, the Oilers won the game 3-2. Lucy and her friend cheered until they had no voice left. It was a fantastic game and even better because the Oilers came out on top.

Reading strategy focus answer: She's happy.

Vocabulary

Stanley Cup: The trophy that the best team in the NHL gets.

NHL: National Hockey League. The highest professional hockey league in Canada and the USA.

jerseys: What sports players wear (or fans).

cheered: Yelled and clapped hands to support a person or team.

tied: The same score (1-1, or 3-3 for example).

goal: Getting a hockey puck in the net. Or, ball in soccer. Used in many other sports too.

Comprehension Questions

1. What is Lucy's favourite hockey team?
2. Why does she like this team?
3. Where does Lucy live now?
4. What is it called when the Calgary Flames and the Edmonton Oilers play each other?
5. How long is a hockey game?
6. Who won the game?

Answers

1. Her favourite hockey team is the Edmonton Oilers.
2. She likes them because she grew up in Edmonton.
3. She lives in Calgary.
4. It's called the Battle of Alberta.
5. It's 60 minutes (3, 20-minute periods).
6. Edmonton won the game.

Synonym Practice: Think of two other words or phrases that have the same meaning as the vocabulary words from the story. Do NOT look at the definitions again, if possible.

1. jersey: _____, _____

2. goal: _____, _____

3. cheer: _____, _____

Summarize the Story

Using 1-2 sentences, summarize the story. Include only the main details and key events.

Summary:

New Words

Write down any new words that you learned from this story. Consider writing them in a vocabulary notebook or making some flashcards for further review.

-

-

-

Let's Talk More

Talk with a friend or classmate about these questions. If you're studying alone, write down 2-3 sentences for each question. There is no correct answer—give your opinion or share your ideas!

1. Have you ever seen an ice hockey game? What did you think about it? If not, what's your favourite sport to watch?

2. Are you a fan of any sports team? Do you have a jersey?

3. In your country, what are some of the most popular sports to play and watch?

4. What are some sports that you know of where people can make physical contact with each other? (like hockey)

Summer Vacation

Reading strategy focus: *Read the title and first paragraph only. Make three predictions about what you think might happen in the story. Write them down. Read the story to see if any of your predictions are correct.*

Ted was a first-year student at the University of Saskatchewan. He had to write his **final exams** at the end of April and then he wouldn't have classes again until September. Most students find summer jobs to make some money during that time. His parents gave him some money for university, but he had to pay for some things like his food and rent himself.

Most of his friends were staying in Saskatoon and finding jobs there. Ted wanted more of an adventure though. He decided to try to find a job in Whistler, British Colombia. It gets busy in the summer with lots of **tourists,** so he thought it shouldn't be difficult. He wanted to get a job there because he loved hiking and other **outdoor activities**. Saskatchewan is quite flat, so he missed the mountains. He also thought that he might meet some interesting people from around the world there. He heard that many Australians worked there.

To find a job, Ted searched the Internet and applied to many different kinds of places. They were mostly jobs in hotels, restaurants, or with tour companies. After a few days, he started to get some phone calls and emails from people who wanted to interview him. He did lots of job interviews, and some of them went well. He hoped someone would offer him a job with **accommodation**. It was difficult and expensive to rent a place in Whistler so most jobs had **staff** housing included. Some places even included meals too.

The following week, he got a phone call from one of the big hotels. They were looking for someone to cut the grass, take out the trash, tidy up the pool area, help carry bags for guests, and other things like that. Best of all, he could stay in a room in the hotel, and they would also provide **meals.** And, if he worked for them for four months, they would pay for his plane ticket from Saskatoon as well. It sounded like a great deal, and he accepted the offer. It was better than other offers, which didn't include a plane ticket or meals. He hoped he'd be able to save at least a **few thousand dollars** for school next year.

He would start on May 1st, just a few days after his last exam. He'd have a lot to organize and of course, he had to study too. But, it would be a fun summer in the mountains!

Vocabulary

final exam: The last test.

tourists: People who travel somewhere for fun.

outdoor activities: Outside things like hiking, cycling, kayaking, etc.

accommodation: A place to stay, overnight.

staff: People who work for a company or organization.

meals: Breakfast, lunch, and dinner.

a few thousand dollars: $3000-5000.

Comprehension Questions

1. How long of a summer break does Ted get?
2. Why does Ted want to work in Whistler?
3. Why is a job with accommodation better?
4. Where did he get a job?
5. Why will he be able to save money?
6. How can he get a free plane ticket?

Answers

1. He gets four months off.
2. He wants to work there because he likes outdoor activities and he wants to meet some interesting people.
3. It's better because accommodation is difficult to find and expensive in Whistler.
4. He got a job at a hotel.
5. He'll be able to save money because meals and accommodation are included.
6. He can get a free plane ticket if he works for four months at the hotel.

Synonym Practice: Think of two other words or phrases that have the same meaning as the vocabulary words from the story. Do NOT look at the definitions again, if possible.

1. staff: _____, _____
2. tourist: _____, _____
3. exam: _____, _____

Summarize the Story

Using 1-2 sentences, summarize the story. Include only the main details and key events.

Summary:

New Words

Write down any new words that you learned from this story. Consider writing them in a vocabulary notebook or making some flashcards for further review.

-

-

-

Let's Talk More

Talk with a friend or classmate about these questions. If you're studying alone, write down 2-3 sentences for each question. There is no correct answer—give your opinion or share your ideas!

1. How long is summer vacation for college or university students in your country? It that a good length of time?
2. Have you ever had a summer job? What did you do?
3. Have you ever moved somewhere for a job?
4. Do you think that Ted will have a good summer? Why or why not?
5. Have you ever had a job that included accommodation or meals?

Applying for University

Reading Strategy Focus: *Look at the questions (see below the story) first. Think about the key words in each question and what kind of information you'll need to find in the story.*

Cindy is in grade 12, which is an important time for Canadian young people! It's the last year of high school, and students have to decide what they want to do when they **graduate**. There are lots of options! Getting a job, going to a **community college**, learning a **trade**, or university. Cindy got good grades in high school, so she decided to go to university. She eventually wanted to be a teacher, so this was necessary.

There are lots of universities in Canada, so she had to decide which ones to apply to. She lived in a small town in Manitoba, but she wanted to go to a bigger city. Her top two choices were Toronto and Vancouver so she applied to the University of Toronto, Simon Fraser University (in Burnbaby, a suburb of Vancouver), and the University of British Columbia (UBC) in Vancouver.

Her first choice was UBC because it had an excellent **education program**, plus Vancouver is an amazing place to live. But, it's also quite difficult to get into UBC because it's **competitive**. You need to get quite high grades in high school in order to even be considered. After she had sent in her applications, she had to wait for a few months to hear back from the universities.

The first school she heard from was the University of Toronto. She didn't get accepted. She felt disappointed and hoped that she would hear better news from the universities in Vancouver. After a few more weeks, she heard from Simon Fraser. Good news! She got in. And then the next day, she also got good news from UBC.

It was an easy decision. UBC! The other good thing about UBC is that they had a new **student residence** where she could get a private room. It was a beautiful new building and each first year student could get their own room. This was much better than Simon Fraser

University where you had to share a room with a roommate. She replied back to UBC and accepted the offer. She told her friends and family members who were all excited for her. Of course, they would miss her, but they were happy that she got into her first choice.

Vocabulary

graduate: Finish an education program.

community college: Like a university but much smaller. Usually has 1-2 year programs.

trade (job): Trade job examples are a plumber, mechanic, carpenter, etc.

education program: Where people who want to be teachers learn to teach.

competitive: Not easy to win. In this case, not easy to get into a certain university.

student residence: A place where university students live, usually on campus.

Comprehension Questions

1. Why is grade 12 important for Canadians?
2. Do all Canadian students go to university?
3. What is Cindy going to do after high school?
4. Where does Cindy want to go to school?
5. Which schools did she get accepted to?
6. Where is she going to study?

Answers

1. It's important because it's the last year of high school and students have to decide what to do after that.
2. No, there are lots of other options besides university.
3. She's going to go to university.
4. She wants to go to a school in Toronto or Vancouver.
5. She got into Simon Fraser University and UBC.
6. She's going to study at UBC.

Synonym Practice: Think of two other words or phrases that have the same meaning as the vocabulary words from the story. Do NOT look at the definitions again, if possible.

1. graduate: _____, _____

2. competitive: _____, _____

3. student residence: _____, _____

Summarize the Story

Using 1-2 sentences, summarize the story. Include only the main details and key events.

Summary:

New Words

Write down any new words that you learned from this story. Consider writing them in a vocabulary notebook or making some flashcards for further review.

-

-

-

Let's Talk More

Talk with a friend or classmate about these questions. If you're studying alone, write down 2-3 sentences for each question. There is no correct answer—give your opinion!

1. What are common things for people to do in your country after high school? What's the best thing in your opinion?

2. What are some positive and negative things about doing a trade? Would you consider doing a trade?

3. Did you go to university or college? How many places did you apply to?

4. In the future, would you prefer to live in a bigger or a smaller city? Why?

Boxing Day Shopping

Reading strategy focus: *Look at the words in **bold**. If you don't know the meaning, make a guess based on the other words in the sentence. Do not use a dictionary. Then, read the questions below and the story.*

In Canada, the day after Christmas (December 26th) is known as Boxing Day. It's similar to Black Friday in the USA. Most people relax at home, eat **leftovers** and play with new things that they got as presents. Some ambitious people clean up everything from Christmas! But, there are also some people that love to shop 'till they drop. Boxing Day usually has the best sales of the year. Some stores even have everything at 50% off regular prices. Some people even get up in the middle of the night to line up outside of **electronics stores**, hoping to get the best deals.

Mel and Cam needed a new TV. Their old one was small, and the picture was **fuzzy**. Plus, the remote control didn't work well, and you had to stand close to the TV to get it to do anything. It was at least 10 years old—neither of them could remember when they bought it. Maybe even closer to 20! So they decided to buy a new one on Boxing Day.

They normally just threw out **flyers** that came to their house without looking at them. But, this time, they had a look at them to see if they could find a deal on a TV. There were a few possibilities that looked good—big enough and for a good price. Then, they did some research online to check reviews for the brand and model.

Mel wanted to buy a TV online and get it delivered. She didn't want to get up early and fight the **crowds** on Boxing Day! You could still get a good deal. But, Cam was convinced that you had to line up early to get the cheapest TV on boxing day. They compared prices. By going to the store, they could save more than a hundred dollars. Finally, Mel agreed.

They enjoyed Christmas with their family and went to bed early. They set their alarm for 4 am before going to sleep. When it went off, it felt like the middle of the night! It basically was. They quickly got up and put some warm clothes on because they'd have to wait outside. They stopped by **Tim Hortons** to get some coffee and muffins to eat while they waited. They arrived at the store, and there were already 20 people in line. They got in line too and prepared to wait until 9 am when the store opened. It was cold, so they took turns sitting in the car with a blanket to get warm. Finally, they got the TV they wanted for a good deal!

Vocabulary

leftovers: Food from a previous meal, that you eat the next day.

electronics store: A place that sells computers, TV's, phones, etc.

fuzzy: Not clear.

flyers: Paper advertisements, usually delivered to a house.

crowd: A lot of people in a location.

Tim Hortons: A famous national coffee chain in Canada.

Comprehension Questions

1. When is Boxing Day?
2. What do people do on Boxing Day?
3. What kind of sales can you find on Boxing Day?
4. How did Mel want to get a new TV?
5. How did Cam want to get a new TV?
6. Why did they have to get up early on Boxing Day?

Answers

1. It's on December 26th.
2. Some people relax, but others go shopping.
3. Almost everything is on sale but some stores have everything for 50% off.
4. She wanted to buy one online.
5. He wanted to get up early and buy one from a store on Boxing Day.
6. They got up early to wait in line at an electronics store.

Synonym Practice: Think of two other words or phrases that have the same meaning as the vocabulary words from the story. Do NOT look at the definitions again, if possible.

1. fuzzy: _____, _____

2. crowd: _____, _____

3. flyers: _____, _____

Summarize the Story

Using 1-2 sentences, summarize the story. Include only the main details and key events.

Summary:

New Words

Write down any new words that you learned from this story. Consider writing them in a vocabulary notebook or making some flashcards for further review.

-

-

-

Let's Talk More

Talk with a friend or classmate about these questions. If you're studying alone, write down 2-3 sentences for each question. There is no correct answer—give your opinion!

1. Do you enjoy shopping? Why or why not?
2. Is there a very popular shopping day in your country? What kinds of deals can you find?
3. What do you think of people who line up all night to get a deal on a TV?
4. Have you ever waited in line for a long time to buy something or get a ticket? Was it worth it?

Online Dating

Reading strategy focus: *Scan the story quickly (set a timer for 30 seconds). Answer this question: Did Sam make his own online dating profile? (yes/no). See answer below the story. Then, read the questions and read the story again, more slowly.*

Sam was feeling sad because his girlfriend had just broken up with him. His friends told him that the best way to get over it would be to meet some new people. They said that he needed to go on some more dates and maybe even meet a new girlfriend. He agreed, but it seemed like a lot of effort to meet someone! These days, he just preferred to stay in his house and watch Netflix!

His friends suggested **online dating,** but he wasn't sure about it. He felt like it would be a weird way to meet a new girlfriend. And what would he write about himself? Which pictures should he choose? He felt uncomfortable even thinking about it, and he'd never tried it before. Sam tried to avoid talking about himself if possible.

Sam and his friends weren't doing much one night. They were just having some beers at one of their houses. His friend Tony said, "Hey, why don't we make you an online dating profile Sam? We can help you!" Sam thought he was joking but Tony was serious. "Give me your phone. I'll do it right now."

Sam thought that he had nothing to lose! His friend Tony **downloaded** the app and started looking through his phone and *Facebook* account for some good pictures. Then, he asked everyone for some words that would describe Sam. They said: **athletic**, funny, kind, adventurous. He asked Sam what his favourite hobbies are. He said: traveling, playing softball, **hanging out with** his dog, and camping.

Tony put it all together into a few sentences and then read it out to everyone. "My friends say that I'm athletic, funny, kind, adventurous and a good catch! You can usually find me traveling, playing softball, camping and hanging out with my dog, Ben. I'm looking for someone who wants to do some of these things with me. Let's chat!"

Sam loved it! Tony published it and gave Sam's phone back to him. He started to see his potential **matches**. He started **swiping right**, which means yes on a few of them. It seemed like there were lots of nice people. Who knows? Maybe he'd meet someone he liked.

Reading strategy focus answer: No

Vocabulary

online dating: Using an app to meet a romantic partner. For example, *Tinder* or *OkCupid*.

downloaded: Got something from the Internet onto your phone, computer or other electronic device.

athletic: A way to describe someone who is good at sports.

hanging out with: Spending time with.

match: On a dating app, describes when both people like each other. Then, you can talk to each other.

swiping right: On a dating app, moving your finger from left to right, which means yes. Swiping left usually means no.

Comprehension Questions

1. Sam felt sad. What advice did his friends give him?
2. Why did he feel sad?
3. Why hadn't Sam tried online dating?
4. Do you think that Tony is a good friend?
5. What did Sam think about his new online dating profile?
6. What does swiping right mean?

Answers

1. They suggested that he meet some new people.
2. His girlfriend has recently broken up with him.
3. He felt uncomfortable about it.
4. (many answers possible). Tony seems like a great friend!
5. He loved his new profile.
6. It means saying "yes" to someone on an online dating app.

Synonym Practice: Think of two other words or phrases that have the same meaning as the vocabulary words from the story. Do NOT look at the definitions again, if possible.

1. athletic: _____, _____
2. hang out: _____, _____
3. swipe right: _____, _____

Summarize the Story

Using 1-2 sentences, summarize the story. Include only the main details and key events.
Summary:

New Words

Write down any new words that you learned from this story. Consider writing them in a vocabulary notebook or making some flashcards for further review.

-

-

-

Let's Talk More

Talk with a friend or classmate about these questions. If you're studying alone, write down 2-3 sentences for each question. There is no correct answer—give your opinion!

1. Have you ever tried online dating? How did it go?
2. Why do you think some people are hesitant to try online dating?
3. What are some things that you *shouldn't* included in an online dating profile? Why?
4. What are some of the advantages and disadvantages of being single and living alone?

Moving Day

Reading strategy focus: *Read the title and first paragraph only. Make three predictions about what you think might happen in the story. Write them down. Read the story to see if any of your predictions are correct.*

Emma didn't like where she lived. She was renting an apartment in Vancouver, which seemed great when she first moved in. However, it was cold in winter, too hot in summer and also **noisy** at night. It seemed like her **upstairs neighbors** didn't sleep at all at night. Instead, they just yelled at each other and walked around. So, she decided to move. She found a new place, not too far away from her current place. The best feature is that it's on the top floor! Hopefully, it would be quieter, and she could sleep well.

Emma had looked into hiring a moving company, but it was expensive—more than $1000! She didn't want to spend that much because she could rent a small truck for the day for less than $100. She would just need some friends to help her. She thought about everyone she knew, and a few people came to mind—the people she played soccer with. They were all athletic and it was a **co-ed team**, so there were lots of men to help with the heavy things.

She sent the team a message, offering to buy dinner and beer for anyone who helped her move. Four people offered. That would be more than enough. Emma was thankful to have such good friends. She **organized** the truck rental and told everyone when and where they should meet.

Before moving day, she was so busy. She organized all of her things, and sold or gave away many of them. She had way too many clothes, books, and dishes. And she tried not to go **grocery shopping** and just eat the food she already had in her freezer and cupboards. Then, she started to **pack** all of her things into suitcases and boxes. It was not an easy job, but she worked on it 1-2 hours a day for about a month. Finally, it was time to move! She was nervous about everything going smoothly.

She got up early and had coffee and breakfast. She knew it would be a long, busy day. Her friends came over and moved the big things first and then the smaller things. It was a big job, but with five people, it went quickly. Thankfully, everything fit into the truck. She slept well on her first night there! It was a good decision to move.

Vocabulary

noisy: Loud.

upstairs neighbors: The people who live above you in an apartment building.

co-ed team: Men and women together on a team.

organized: Arranged.

grocery shopping: Buying food in a store.

pack: Put things into a box or suitcase to go somewhere else.

Comprehension Questions

1. Why did Emma want to move?
2. Why didn't Emma hire a moving company?
3. Who did Emma ask to help her move?
4. What did Emma give away or sell?
5. How long did it take her to pack?
6. How did moving go?

Answers

1. She wanted to move because it was noisy at her place and difficult to sleep. It was also too hot and too cold.
2. The moving company was too expensive.
3. She asked her soccer teammates.
4. She sold or gave away many clothes, books, and dishes.
5. It took her about a month to pack.
6. It went well.

Synonym Practice: Think of two other words or phrases that have the same meaning as the vocabulary words from the story. Do NOT look at the definitions again, if possible.

1. noisy: _____, _____

2. organize: _____, _____

3. pack: _____, _____

Summarize the Story

Using 1-2 sentences, summarize the story. Include only the main details and key events.

Summary:

New Words

Write down any new words that you learned from this story. Consider writing them in a vocabulary notebook or making some flashcards for further review.

-

-

-

Let's Talk More

Talk with a friend or classmate about these questions. If you're studying alone, write down 2-3 sentences for each question. There is no correct answer—give your opinion or share your ideas!

1. Do you know how many times you've moved in your life? What are some reasons why you moved?

2. Have you ever gotten friends to help you move? How did you "pay" them?

3. Moving is one of the most stressful human experiences. Why do think this is?

4. Have you ever had to move because of bad neighbors? Or, know someone who did? Share the story.

Tennis Lessons

Reading Strategy Focus: *Look at the questions (see below the story) first. Think about the key words in each question and what kind of information you'll need to find in the story.*

Tom had always wanted to learn how to play tennis. Some of his friends played and he asked them to play with him. They asked if he'd ever played before. He said no, but that he had a racket and some balls. They said no. They only liked to play with people who could play well—people who could hit the ball back and forth at least 10 times in a row. But, they recommended that he take some tennis lessons and then they could play together.

He searched on the Internet and found some indoor and outdoor lessons. The outdoor ones were cheaper but could be **cancelled** if it was raining. The indoor ones were more expensive but couldn't be cancelled due to rain. He decided to **sign up** for a 10-week, indoor program that would start in a few weeks. There were some shorter lessons of only four weeks, but he decided to take the longer ones because he wanted lots of opportunities to practice.

During the first lesson, he met his coach Amy and classmates. There were four of them in the class, and they'd all be playing together on the same court. Everyone seemed nice and excited about learning how to play tennis.

During the first lesson, they learned how to hold the racket **properly**. Tom learned that you had to change your **tennis grip** when you hit a forehand and then change it slightly when you hit a backhand. He found the forehand much easier than the backhand shot. Amy was patient and hit hundreds of balls to them so they could practice their strokes. They all improved quickly with her tips and coaching.

In the following lessons, they learned the rules of tennis and basic **positioning**. They also learned how to **serve**. You get two chances to serve in tennis. Your first serve should be harder because it doesn't matter if you miss. Then, your second serve should never miss, or you'll lose the point. They even played some games with the four students while Amy gave them advice and helped them keep score.

After the ten weeks, Tom asked his friends to play. They agreed, and they were surprised by his skill level! Tom was so happy that he'd taken lessons. Now, he could play tennis regularly with his friend. He was excited for summer to come so he could play outside.

Vocabulary

cancelled: Something won't happen. In this case, an outdoor tennis lesson if it's raining.

sign up: Join; register.

properly: The correct way.

tennis grip: How you hold a tennis racket.

positioning: Where to stand. In this case, where to stand while playing tennis.

serve: Putting the ball in play in some sports or starting the point. Tennis and volleyball, for example.

Comprehension Questions

1. Why didn't Tom's friends want to play tennis with him?
2. What advice did his friends give him?
3. What are the advantages and disadvantages of indoor lessons?
4. Who is Amy?
5. What did Tom's friends think about his tennis skills after the lessons?
6. Was Tom happy that he took the lessons?

Answers

1. They didn't want to play with him because he didn't know how to play tennis.
2. They told him to take lessons.
3. They are expensive but couldn't be cancelled because of bad weather.
4. Amy is Tom's tennis coach.
5. They thought he played well.
6. Yes, he was.

Synonym Practice: Think of two other words or phrases that have the same meaning as the vocabulary words from the story. Do NOT look at the definitions again, if possible.

1. sign up: _____, _____

2. cancel: _____, _____

3. properly: _____, _____

Summarize the Story

Using 1-2 sentences, summarize the story. Include only the main details and key events.

Summary:

New Words

Write down any new words that you learned from this story. Consider writing them in a vocabulary notebook or making some flashcards for further review.

-

-

-

Let's Talk More

Talk with a friend or classmate about these questions. If you're studying alone, write down 2-3 sentences for each question. There is no correct answer—give your opinion or share your ideas!

1. Have you ever taken some sports lessons? How did it go?

2. Do you think tennis would be a fun sport to play? Why or why not?

3. What do you think of Tom's friends who wouldn't play with him because he was a beginner?

4. Have you learned any new sport or skill lately? What is it?

Thanksgiving Dinner

Reading strategy focus: *Scan the story quickly (set a timer for 30 seconds). Answer this question: Did the family meet in person or online this year for Thanksgiving? See answer below the story. Then, read the questions and read the story again, more slowly.*

Kim's favourite holiday is Thanksgiving. She loves the food, getting together with family and the changing colours of the leaves. In Canada, Thanksgiving is in October, instead of November like in the USA.

When she was a kid, Kim's grandmother used to cook a big feast that included turkey, ham, **stuffing**, mashed potatoes, sweet potatoes, salads, and pumpkin pie with whipped cream. The adults would have wine, and the kids would have pop. She would eat until she was **stuffed** and then eat a little bit more after that! But her favourite thing was playing with all of her cousins. She'd usually only see them at Thanksgiving, Christmas, and Easter—the biggest holidays in Canada.

When Kim got older, she still enjoyed Thanksgiving with friends and family. Sometimes she'd cook the turkey. It was a big responsibility! You had to take it out of the fridge to **thaw** for a few days. Then, you had to cook it for hours, making sure it was cooked in the middle but not burnt on the outside. There are lots of different ways to season the turkey and everyone has a secret recipe. It isn't easy but everyone said that Kim did a great job with it!

During Covid, Thanksgiving looked a little bit different. Her family members all cooked their own meals at home. The usual things—mashed potatoes with gravy, stuffing, and veggies. Except most people cooked a small chicken instead of turkey. Turkeys are big and are best for at least 10 people. Then, everyone ate together while on a Zoom call. It was a little bit different but still nice to see everyone. They **chatted** for hours and only said goodbye when it started to get late and everyone wanted to clean up all the food and do the dishes. Kim was starting to get sleepy from drinking lots of wine too!

Whether in person or on *Zoom*, one of Kim's favourite **traditions** was for everyone to say what they're thankful for that year. This year, everyone was thankful to be healthy and safe. Others were thankful to have a job and a nice place to live.

Reading strategy focus answer: They met online.

Vocabulary

stuffing: Bread with spices, vegetables, butter, etc. that is cooked inside of a turkey.

stuffed: Very full.

thaw: Become not frozen.

chatted: Talked.

traditions: Things that you do every year, usually to celebrate a holiday.

Comprehension Questions

1. Are Canadian and American Thanksgivings on the same day?

2. What are some foods that people eat at Thanksgiving?

3. Why was Thanksgiving different this year?

4. How much does Kim usually eat at Thanksgiving?

5. Is Kim good at cooking turkey?

6. What is one of Kim's favourite Thanksgiving traditions?

Answers

1. No, they aren't. Canadian Thanksgiving is in October while American Thanksgiving is in November.

2. People eat turkey and gravy, mashed potatoes, ham, stuffing, vegetables, sweet potatoes, and pumpkin pie.

3. It was different because of Covid.

4. She eats a lot until she's stuffed.

5. Yes, she's good at it.

6. One of her favourite traditions is saying what everyone is thankful for.

Synonym Practice: Think of two other words or phrases that have the same meaning as the vocabulary words from the story. Do NOT look at the definitions again, if possible.

1. chat: _____, _____
2. stuffed: _____, _____
3. thaw: _____, _____

Summarize the Story

Using 1-2 sentences, summarize the story. Include only the main details and key events.

Summary:

New Words

Write down any new words that you learned from this story. Consider writing them in a vocabulary notebook or making some flashcards for further review.

-

-

-

Let's Talk More

Talk with a friend or classmate about these questions. If you're studying alone, write down 2-3 sentences for each question. There is no correct answer—give your opinion!

1. What's your favourite holiday? Why? How do you celebrate?
2. Have you ever been to a Canadian or American Thanksgiving celebration? How was it?
3. Have you celebrated holidays differently because of Covid-19? How?
4. What are some things that you're thankful for?
5. Does your country have a kind of Thanksgiving/harvest/fall celebration? What is it?

There's a Bear!

Reading strategy focus: *Look at the words in **bold**. If you don't know the meaning, make a guess based on the other words in the sentence. Do not use a dictionary. Then, read the questions below and the story.*

Port Coquitlam is a **suburb** of Vancouver. It's known as the home of Terry Fox, a well-known Canadian **hero** who raised a lot of money for cancer research. But, it's also known as a place that has a lot of bears. They like Port Coquitlam so much because there's a lot to eat. There are **salmonberries** in the spring, and blackberries and blueberries later in the summer. In the fall, the bears **gorge** themselves on salmon, getting fat for their winter **hibernation**.

Tommy had just moved to Port Coquitlam with his wife and two kids. They lived in a neighborhood that was next to a small **stream**. There were lots of delicious things for the bears to eat there—salmonberries and salmon, so they'd often see bears in their neighborhood. Usually, the bears were just looking for food and didn't bother the people. And the people didn't bother the bears as well. But, you had to be careful with your trash and keep it locked up.

One day, they were eating breakfast when one of his kids said, "Dad! There's a bear outside." Tommy thought she was joking, so he just laughed. But his daughter said it again! Everyone looked outside the window, and there was a small bear walking along the fence. Even a small bear is quite big! It was impressive how good at balancing the bear was. Tommy felt a bit nervous and hoped that the bear wouldn't come closer to their house.

They watched carefully. The bear was **sniffing** the air. He was probably looking for something to eat. Maybe some vegetables in a garden or some trash that someone left out. Then the bear jumped into their neighbor's yard and started sniffing a BBQ that they had out. The bear didn't find anything interesting and then jumped back onto the fence and into a front yard. They ran to another window in their house to see if they could still see it. Sure enough, it was walking down the street, sniffing the air again. Surprised people in cars stopped to watch.

It was just a normal day in Port Coquitlam!

Vocabulary

suburb: A smaller city or community outside of a big city.

hero: Someone that many people look up to.

salmonberry: A kind of berry that grows on the West coast of the USA and Canada.

gorge: Eat a lot.

hibernation: Bears sleeping for the winter months.

stream: Like a river but much smaller.

sniffing: Smelling.

Comprehension Questions

1. Where is Port Coquitlam located?
2. What is Port Coquitlam famous for?
3. Why do bears like Port Coquitlam so much?
4. Why do bears eat a lot of salmon?
5. Do bears attack people in Port Coquitlam?
6. Why did some people in cars stop?

Answers

1. It's located close to Vancouver.
2. It's the home of a Canadian hero, Terry Fox.
3. They like it because there's a lot to eat there.
4. They eat a lot of salmon because they're getting ready for hibernation.
5. No, they don't. They're usually just looking for food.
6. They stopped because they were surprised to see a bear walking down the street.

Synonym Practice: Think of two other words or phrases that have the same meaning as the vocabulary words from the story. Do NOT look at the definitions again, if possible.

1. sniff: _____, _____

2. stream: _____, _____

3. hero: _____, _____

Summarize the Story

Using 1-2 sentences, summarize the story. Include only the main details and key events.

Summary:

New Words

Write down any new words that you learned from this story. Consider writing them in a vocabulary notebook or making some flashcards for further review.

-

-

-

Let's Talk More

Talk with a friend or classmate about these questions. If you're studying alone, write down 2-3 sentences for each question. There is no correct answer—give your opinion or share your ideas!

1. What would you do if you saw a bear in your backyard? Why?
2. Have you ever seen wild animals some place where they shouldn't be?
3. Are there any dangerous animals in your country?
4. What are some of the positive and negative things about living in a suburb?

What's that Noise?

Reading Strategy Focus: *Look at the questions (see below the story) first. Think about the key words in each question and what kind of information you'll need to find in the story.*

Terry had recently moved to Vancouver from Manitoba and was learning about all things British Columbia. Life **on the coast** was quite a bit different than on the **prairies**. But she loved it so far. The weather wasn't as cold, even though it does rain a lot. And there are lots of mountains and the ocean to enjoy. She was looking forward to trying snowboarding in Whistler after it snowed. And who doesn't enjoy fresh, cheap sushi on almost every single street corner?

Terry's friend Samantha asked her to go for a walk. It was a beautiful fall day in November. Beautiful for that time of year in Vancouver means sunny and not raining. It rains a lot in Vancouver during the winter!

They were walking beside a stream when Terry heard a noise. It was unlike anything she'd ever heard before. It sounded like people were **slapping** the water with their hands. "That's so strange," she thought to herself, "Why would people do that?" Who's in the water at this time of year? It's so cold.

She asked Samantha what the strange noise was. She laughed and said, "Oh! That's right. You're from Manitoba and don't know about this. It's the salmon."

"What do you mean? Salmon? I've never heard about this," Terry said.

Samantha explained all about Salmon to her. They are born in small streams like the one they were walking beside. They spend time in the streams until they're big enough, and then they go out into the Pacific Ocean. Sometimes, they travel thousands of kilometers in search of food. Salmon are an important food for killer whales in the area. When they **mature** at about seven years old, they travel back to the river or stream they were born in to lay eggs. Most salmon die after laying eggs.

Terry asked what happens to salmon who return to their birth stream to find that it's too dirty or polluted? Samantha said that they probably won't lay eggs there, and there will be fewer salmon in the future. And that it's the reason why it's so important to protect our streams from pollution. She said that we need to dispose of things like paint properly and also be careful with **pesticides** and **fertilizers** that we use.

Vocabulary

on the coast: Next to the ocean

prairies: In Canada, refers to the middle, flat provinces (Alberta, Saskatchewan, and Manitoba).

slapping: Hitting.

mature: Fully developed.

pesticides: Chemicals used to kill weeds/unwanted plants.

fertilizers: Chemicals used to help things grow well.

Comprehension Questions

1. Did Terry like living in Vancouver?
2. Why didn't Terry know about salmon?
3. Where are salmon born?
4. Where do salmon go once they're big enough?
5. Where do salmon go to lay eggs?
6. How can we protect rivers and streams?

Answers

1. Yes, she did.
2. She didn't know about salmon because there aren't any in Manitoba.
3. They are born in small streams and rivers.
4. They go into the ocean.
5. They return to the river or stream where they were born to lay eggs.
6. We should be careful about what we put into streams and avoid things like paint, pesticides, and fertilizers.

Synonym Practice: Think of two other words or phrases that have the same meaning as the

vocabulary words from the story. Do NOT look at the definitions again, if possible.

1. slap: _____, _____
2. mature: _____, _____
3. pesticides: _____, _____

Summarize the Story

Using 1-2 sentences, summarize the story. Include only the main details and key events.

Summary:

New Words

Write down any new words that you learned from this story. Consider writing them in a vocabulary notebook or making some flashcards for further review.

-
-
-

Let's Talk More

Talk with a friend or classmate about these questions. If you're studying alone, write down 2-3 sentences for each question. There is no correct answer—give your opinion or share your ideas!

1. Do you think it's important to protect the environment, including streams and rivers?
2. Have you ever seen something like salmon returning to where they were born?
3. What are some things that you do to protect the environment?
4. Have you ever moved to a place that was very different from where you grew up? What are some of the first things you noticed about your new place?

73

Canadian Football

Reading strategy focus: *Look at the words in* **bold**. *If you don't know the meaning, make a guess based on the other words in the sentence. Do not use a dictionary. Then, read the questions below and the story.*

Everyone in North America probably knows the NFL (The National Football League) and teams like the Dallas Cowboys. American rules football is famous in the USA and around the world. Unfortunately, there are no Canadian teams in the NFL. This is different from the NBA (basketball), MLB (baseball), and NHL (hockey) which have many American teams but a few Canadian teams as well.

However, Canada has its own league, the CFL (The Canadian Football League). It's **quite similar** to the NFL except for a few things. The **field** size is bigger in the CFL, but there's also one more player on the field. And in the CFL, you have three "downs" instead of four like in the NFL. A down means a chance to run or throw the ball **10 yards**. If you don't get a down, the other team gets the ball back.

The CFL season starts in August and then ends with the Grey Cup between the best two teams in December. Kevin and his friend Bob are huge fans of the Saskatchewan Roughriders and have **season tickets**. This means that they get tickets to all of the **home games**. It's fun in August and September when the weather is good but then it starts to get colder from October onwards. Sometimes, it's even snowing during a game, but it would never get cancelled!

At the games later in the year, people wear their winter clothing—heavy jackets, boots, scarves, mitts, and **toques**. Some people even bring **sleeping bags** or blankets to the games to help them stay warm. Instead of drinking beer like in the summer, people drink warm drinks like coffee or tea to help them warm up. You can sometimes see people jumping up and down and moving their arms to try to stay warm!

Part of the fun for Kevin and Bob is cheering for the Roughriders, even when they are losing. The other part is surviving the cold and bad weather. All of their coworkers and friends talk about how good of fans they are for going to the games, no matter what. They are impressed at how they can handle the cold. Kevin always says, "You're not Canadian until you've watched a CFL game in the snow!" He often invites his coworkers to the games, but they always say no to the winter ones!

Vocabulary

quite similar: Almost the same.

field: A large area outside where people play sports.

10 yards: 9.1 meters.

season tickets: Tickets for all the home games for a sports team.

home games: When a sports team plays in the city that they're from. For example, when the Edmonton Oilers play a game in Edmonton.

toque: A Canadian word for a warm winter hat.

sleeping bags: Used for camping to sleep in to stay warm.

Comprehension Questions

1. What's the CFL? The NFL?
2. Who are the Dallas Cowboys?
3. Are the rules the same for the CFL and NFL?
4. Why is it more fun to watch football in August or September?
5. Do CFL games get cancelled if it's snowing?
6. How do people stay warm at the games in winter?

Answers

1. CFL = Canadian Football League. All the teams are in Canada. NFL = National Football League. All the teams are in the USA.
2. They are a famous NFL team.
3. No, there are some differences. For example, 3 vs 4 downs.
4. It's more fun because the weather is better in Canada.
5. No, they play in the snow.
6. They wear warm clothes and drink warm things.

Synonym Practice: Think of two other words or phrases that have the same meaning as the vocabulary words from the story. Do NOT look at the definitions again, if possible.

1. toque: _____, _____
2. field: _____, _____
3. similar: _____, _____

Summarize the Story

Using 1-2 sentences, summarize the story. Include only the main details and key events.

Summary:

New Words

Write down any new words that you learned from this story. Consider writing them in a vocabulary notebook or making some flashcards for further review.

-
-
-

Let's Talk More

Talk with a friend or classmate about these questions. If you're studying alone, write down 2-3 sentences for each question. There is no correct answer—give your opinion!

1. Have you ever watched an American or Canadian football game? What did you think?
2. Would you ever go to a sports game when it's snowing?
3. Have you ever been to a sports event in person? How was it?
4. What do you think of Kevin and Bob?
5. Do you think that professional sports players make too much money? Why or why not?

It's so Cold!

Reading strategy focus: *Scan the story quickly (set a timer for 30 seconds). Answer this question: How does Kara get to school in the winter? (bus, walk or, bike). See answer below the story. Then, read the questions and read the story again, more slowly.*

Kara recently moved to Winnipeg from Kelowna to go to the University of Manitoba. She rented a small apartment with some other students not too far away from **campus.** She started classes in September and used to walk or ride her bicycle to school. Walking took about an hour, but she would listen to some **audiobooks**, which made the time go by quickly. Riding her bike was much faster—only 10 minutes, and she'd do that if it wasn't raining.

Once the weather started to get cold, she began taking the bus. It wasn't so bad. The bus stop was about only five minutes from her house, and the bus to the university came every 10 or 15 minutes during peak times. She was often lucky and could get a seat too. Even standing wasn't that bad because it was such a short trip.

For **Christmas break**, she went back to visit her parents and friends in Kelowna. Then, she flew back to Winnipeg. As soon as she stepped out of the airport, she knew things were different! It was so cold and so windy. No amount of clothes could keep you warm in weather like that. She was thankful she had her winter jacket, gloves, and hat with her. She decided to take a taxi to her apartment because it was too cold to wait for the bus and it was annoying, with her big suitcase.

She checked the **weather forecast** for the following week when she got home. -35 to -40 degrees **Celsius**. And windy as well. She'd never experienced weather like that before and had no idea what to expect. But she had to get to her classes, and it would be too expensive to take a taxi to school every day. She'd just have to dress more warmly and take the bus. The worst thing would be waiting at the bus stop.

The next morning, she got up, took a shower and ate some breakfast. Then, she put on her warmest **leggings**, jeans, and thick socks. She wore a long sleeve shirt, sweater and got her warmest winter jacket out. She found a toque, gloves and scarf. Kara put everything on, took a deep breath and stepped outside. It was almost like she was wearing nothing. The cold took her breath away!

Reading strategy focus answer: She takes the bus in winter.

Vocabulary

campus: A name for a location where a university or college is.

audiobook: A book that you can listen to.

Christmas break: A vacation that students and employees get in December/early January.

weather forecast: Prediction for the weather (temperature, rain, snow, etc.).

Celsius: A way to measure temperature in Canada and in most other countries around the world.

leggings: A kind of tight pants.

Comprehension Questions

1. Is Kelowna warmer or colder than Winnipeg?
2. How does she get to school when the weather is good?
3. What does Kara do while walking to school?
4. Did she like taking the bus to school?
5. How did she prepare for the cold weather?
6. What happened when she went outside on the very cold morning?

Answers

1. Kelowna is warmer. Kara had never experienced such cold temperatures.
2. She walks or rides her bike.
3. She listens to audiobooks.
4. Taking the bus was okay, except when it was very cold out.
5. She prepared by dressing warmly.
6. She felt cold and also like she couldn't breathe.

Synonym Practice: Think of two other words or phrases that have the same meaning as the vocabulary words from the story. Do NOT look at the definitions again, if possible.

1. campus: _____, _____
2. leggings: _____, _____

Summarize the Story

Using 1-2 sentences, summarize the story. Include only the main details and key events.

Summary:

New Words

Write down any new words that you learned from this story. Consider writing them in a vocabulary notebook or making some flashcards for further review.

-

-

-

Let's Talk More

Talk with a friend or classmate about these questions. If you're studying alone, write down 2-3 sentences for each question. There is no correct answer—give your opinion or share your ideas!

1. How do you get to work or school? Does this change, depending on the weather?
2. Have you ever experienced very cold temperatures? When and where?
3. Have you ever experienced very hot temperatures? When and where?
4. Do you prefer the hot or cold, if you have a choice?
5. Would you ever move to a place where is was sometimes -40 C? Why or why not?

Christmas in May

Reading Strategy Focus: *Read the title and first paragraph only. Make three predictions about what you think might happen in the story. Write them down. Read the story to see if any of your predictions are correct.*

Sam was hanging out with his friend Carrie in Burnaby, a suburb of Vancouver. They were at Deer Lake, a popular park. Sam and Carrie were walking around the lake, enjoying a beautiful spring day, when they saw **a bunch** of trucks, equipment, and people. It was quite unusual to see something like that at a public park. "I wonder what this is?," said Sam. "I'm not sure, let's take a closer look," replied Carrie.

So they went to check it out but were soon stopped by a person with a **walkie-talkie**. "You can't come into this area," said the person. Sam and Carrie asked that person what was going on. The person said that they were filming a movie. There are lots of TV shows and movies filmed in Vancouver, so it wasn't so unusual to see this. They asked the person which movie they were filming, and she said that it was a "**made for TV movie**." She also mentioned that it wasn't something they would have heard of.

Sam was still curious about it and wondered if anyone famous was in the movie that he might recognize. He suggested walking around the fence that blocked off access to the set to see if they could get a better look. They walked for a minute or two and then started to see an unusual scene—lots of snow, Christmas lights and other Christmas decorations. The set was a small town designed to look like it was winter, even though May is springtime in Canada. It looked realistic, and they were impressed at how well done it was.

They **peered** through the fence, trying to catch **a glimpse** of the **stars**. But, they could only see lots of cables, crew members, cameras, makeup artists, hair stylists, a snack table and things like that. They couldn't see any actors or actresses. It actually looked like everyone was setting up because they didn't hear a director yelling things like action or cut. They took a few pictures and continued their walk. It was an interesting experience for them, but they were a little bit disappointed not to see any famous people.

Vocabulary

a bunch = Many; a lot of.

walkie-talkies: Radios that people use to talk to each other.

made for TV movie: A movie that never plays in movie theaters. Instead, it goes directly to TV or online streaming websites.

peered: Looked closely.

a **glimpse:** A brief look at something.

stars: In this situation, refers to actors or actresses.

Comprehension Questions

1. What season is it in May in Canada?

2. Was the snow that they saw real?

3. Did the Christmas scene look real?

4. Did Sam and Carrie see any actors or actresses?

5. Could they go onto the set?

6. What were they disappointed about?

Answers

1. It's spring.

2. No, the snow was fake.

3. Yes, it looked quite realistic.

4. No, they didn't.

5. No, they couldn't. They had to look at it through a fence.

6. They hoped to see some stars.

Synonym Practice: Think of two other words or phrases that have the same meaning as the vocabulary words from the story. Do NOT look at the definitions again, if possible.

1. a bunch: _____, _____

2. peer: _____, _____

3. star: _____, _____

Summarize the Story

Using 1-2 sentences, summarize the story. Include only the main details and key events.

Summary:

New Words

Write down any new words that you learned from this story. Consider writing them in a vocabulary notebook or making some flashcards for further review.

-

-

-

Let's Talk More

Talk with a friend or classmate about these questions. If you're studying alone, write down 2-3 sentences for each question. There is no correct answer—give your opinion or share your ideas!

1. Have you ever seen a TV or movie show being made? What did you think?

2. Have you ever met anyone famous? If not, would you like to?

3. Are there any TV shows or movies filmed in your city? Where are they usually filmed?

Vancouver Sushi

Reading strategy focus: *Look at the words in **bold**. If you don't know the meaning, make a guess based on the other words in the sentence. Do not use a dictionary. Then, read the questions below and the story.*

Sid came to Canada from India for university. He was studying business at Simon Fraser University in Burnaby, a suburb of Vancouver. It was an entirely different world than his home in India, and he spent the first few weeks discovering the parks, shops, and restaurants around where he lived. He loved the cheap pizza place, a nice Italian restaurant and a taco shop. Most of the people in his neighborhood were students so the restaurants had **big portions** for **a good price**.

Sid noticed a lot of sushi restaurants. Being a **vegetarian**, he didn't eat meat, so he didn't try them because he didn't want to eat raw fish. In fact, he'd never tried sushi in his entire life, and he thought that he probably wouldn't like it. It wasn't popular in India at all.

In one of his classes, Sid sat beside a Canadian student named Chris. They had a few classes together and started to sit together in most of them. They **chatted** before and after class most days. On Fridays, they had an **economics** class that ended at 1:00 and then they were finished for the day.

Chris suggested that they go out for some sushi at a place on campus. Sid said that he'd love to get lunch but that he didn't eat fish. Chris laughed and said, "Sid! That's no problem. There are lots of things you can eat at a sushi restaurant, even if you're a vegetarian. Have you ever had sushi before?" Sid told him that he hadn't. Chris reassured him that he'd probably like it and to give it a try.

So they headed to the sushi restaurant, and Sid took a look at the menu. Most things were unfamiliar to him and had Japanese names. Chris noticed the confused look on his face and suggested some things that he could try if he didn't want to eat meat or fish. He suggested trying a yam roll, avocado roll, cucumber roll, agedashi tofu, miso soup, and gomae (spinach salad). Sid said that it all sounded great but he wasn't sure what to choose. Chris said, let's get them all and share! My treat. Sid loved it and found his new **addiction**!

Vocabulary

big portion: A large serving of food.

a good price: Reasonable price for something.

vegetarian: Someone who doesn't eat meat but does eat eggs and dairy products.

chatted: Talked.

economics: The study of production (making things), consumption (buying things) and wealth/money.

addiction: A way to describe something that you can't stop doing. In this case, eating sushi.

Comprehension Questions

1. Does Sid enjoy eating out?
2. Why had Sid never tried sushi?
3. How did Sid meet Chris?
4. Why did Sid agree to get sushi?
5. What did Sid get to eat?
6. Did Sid like sushi?

Answers

1. Yes, he does.
2. It wasn't popular in India, and he thought it was all raw fish.
3. They had some classes together at university.
4. Sid agreed because Chris told him that there are lots of options besides raw fish.
5. Sid and Chris shared all the things that Chris suggested to him.
6. Yes, he loved it.

Synonym Practice: Think of two other words or phrases that have the same meaning as the vocabulary words from the story. Do NOT look at the definitions again, if possible.

1. chat: _____, _____

2. a good price: _____, _____

Summarize the Story

Using 1-2 sentences, summarize the story. Include only the main details and key events.

Summary:

New Words

Write down any new words that you learned from this story. Consider writing them in a vocabulary notebook or making some flashcards for further review.

-

-

-

Let's Talk More

Talk with a friend or classmate about these questions. If you're studying alone, write down 2-3 sentences for each question. There is no correct answer—give your opinion!

1. Have you ever tried sushi? What did you think?

2. Are you adventurous when it comes to trying new kinds of food?

3. Would you ever consider becoming a vegetarian? Why or why not?

4. Do you like trying new restaurants or do you prefer to stick with a few that you already know?

What's That?

Reading strategy focus: *Scan the story quickly (set a timer for 30 seconds). Answer this question: What was the unusual thing they saw on the hike? See answer below the story. Then, read the questions and read the story again, more slowly.*

Sam and Carla were old friends and decided to take a trip to the Sunshine Coast on a long weekend in October. To get there, you have to take a **ferry** from Vancouver. It's short though—only about 40 minutes by boat from Horseshoe Bay, where the ferry terminal is. They decided to stay in a cute cabin in the forest.

Sam's coworker grew up on the sunshine coast, so she asked her for some travel advice about things they should see, do, and eat. Sam's coworker said that her favourite hike was Skookumchuck Narrows, a beautiful hike through the rainforest that ended at a spectacular scene. It's where the ocean rushes through a narrow spot at **high tide and low tide**, creating a lot of rushing water. At low tide, you could see **whirlpools,** and at high tide, you could see **rapids** that kayakers liked to play in. It sounded so interesting and like a must-see thing!

Sam and Carla both thought it sounded great, so they checked the **tide tables**. High tide was at 3:00 on Saturday afternoon, so they agreed to aim for that time. They woke up on Saturday morning to lots of rain! But, they put on their rain gear and decided to do it anyways. Most of the hike was under the trees, so they hoped that they wouldn't get too wet.

After about an hour of hiking, they reached the rapids and hung out for a while, watching the kayakers having some fun. Then, Carla saw an unusual movement in the water. It looked like a big animal was playing in the rapids too. She tried to point it out to Sam, but it slipped under the water. Finally, it came to the surface again! It was a sea lion, a massive animal. It was playing in the water, having fun, just like the kayakers.

They both tried to take pictures and video, but it was quite difficult. The sea lion was

elusive! They'd just have to remember this amazing sight in their minds. Finally, the graceful animal disappeared, and they hiked back to their car. All they wanted was a hot shower and cup of tea after being out in the rain for so long. But, it was totally worth it!

Reading strategy focus answer: A sea lion.

Vocabulary

ferry: A boat that people use for transportation purposes.

high tide/low tide: Refers to water levels of the ocean, on a daily basis. They are affected by the moon.

whirlpool: Water moving in a circular motion.

rapids: A fast-flowing section of water, usually in a river. In this case, it's referring to the ocean.

tide table: A chart that tells you when high and low tide are.

elusive: Difficult to find or see.

Comprehension Questions

1. How can you get to the Sunshine Coast from Vancouver?
2. How did Sam find out about this hike?
3. Should you hike the Skookumchuck Narrows at a specific time?
4. How was the weather on Saturday?
5. What did they expect to see in the rapids?
6. What was the surprising thing they saw in the rapids?

Answers

1. You have to take a short ferry ride.
2. Sam's co-worker told her about the hike.
3. The best time is at high or low tide.
4. It was rainy.
5. They expected to see people kayaking.
6. The surprising thing they saw was a sea lion.

Synonym Practice: Think of two other words or phrases that have the same meaning as the vocabulary words from the story. Do NOT look at the definitions again, if possible.

1. ferry: _____, _____
2. elusive: _____, _____
3. rapids: _____, _____

Summarize the Story

Using 1-2 sentences, summarize the story. Include only the main details and key events.

Summary:

New Words

Write down any new words that you learned from this story. Consider writing them in a vocabulary notebook or making some flashcards for further review.

-

-

-

Let's Talk More

Talk with a friend or classmate about these questions. If you're studying alone, write down 2-3 sentences for each question. There is no correct answer—give your opinion or share your ideas!

1. Have you ever seen something surprising that you didn't expect to see?
2. Have you ever gone on a very rainy hike? How was it?
3. Have you ever cancelled a plan because of bad weather? What was it?
4. What was the last trip you went on? Describe it.

Halloween

Lauren had recently moved to Toronto from Shanghai for work. One of her coworkers, Sarah asked what she was doing for **Halloween** in a few days. Lauren said that she wasn't doing much and that she honestly didn't even know that much about Halloween. People in China didn't celebrate it, except for some **expats** who would dress up and go out to bars. She'd certainly never done anything to celebrate it.

Sarah had a look of horror on her face! She said that it's the best holiday and her personal favourite because it's just about having fun. She couldn't believe that Lauren had never celebrated it before. Lauren said that she'd probably hand out candy at her house but that she didn't know how many kids would come because it was mostly adults where she lived. She hoped some kids would come so she didn't have to eat all the candy herself! She was trying to cut back on how much junk food she ate!

Sarah, who had two young kids, said that Lauren should come hang out with them and take the kids **trick-or-treating** with her. She told Lauren about the plan. Lauren should come over after work for an early dinner at around 5:30. Dinner was lots of healthy things since the kids would eat so much junk food later. Then, everyone would put on their costumes, get their candy sacks (an old pillowcase) and wait until around 6:30. Sarah's husband would stay home this year to hand out candy. The adults usually bring an alcoholic drink in a travel mug! Then, the kids **rush** from house to house, knocking on doors to get candy!

Lauren said that it sounded fun and that she'd join them. But, she wondered about a costume. Did adults **dress up** too? Sarah said that it was up to her. Maybe 1/3 of the adults who take their kids trick or treating dress up. Lauren said that she'd like to have the full experience so she'd do some research online and find something fun. Sarah mentioned a Halloween store in Toronto, not far from their work that has so many costumes and recommended going there. Now, the only thing left to do was wait for Halloween to come!

Vocabulary

Halloween: A popular holiday in North America on October 31st.

expats (expatriates): People who live in a different country for a period of time, other than the one of their birth.

trick-or-treating: What kids do on Halloween. They go to houses and ask for a treat (candy) or they'll do a trick.

rush: Move quickly; hurry.

dress up: Put on a costume (Halloween or costume party) or wear formal clothes (wedding, etc.).

Comprehension Questions

1. Why didn't Lauren know that much about Halloween?
2. How did Lauren and Sarah know each other?
3. Who is going trick-or-treating?
4. Why does Sarah feed her kid a healthy dinner on Halloween?
5. What did adults often bring trick-or-treating?
6. Where did Sarah recommend getting a costume from?

Answers

1. She didn't know that much because it's not a popular holiday in China.
2. They are coworkers.
3. Sarah, her two kids, and Lauren are going trick-or-treating.
4. She feeds her kids a healthy dinner because they'll eat lots of junk food later.
5. They often bring an alcoholic drink.
6. She recommended that Lauren check out the big Halloween store near their work.

Synonym Practice: Think of two other words or phrases that have the same meaning as the

vocabulary words from the story. Do NOT look at the definitions again, if possible.

1. rush: _____, _____
2. dress up: _____, _____

Summarize the Story

Using 1-2 sentences, summarize the story. Include only the main details and key events.

Summary:

New Words

Write down any new words that you learned from this story. Consider writing them in a vocabulary notebook or making some flashcards for further review.

-

-

-

Let's Talk More

Talk with a friend or classmate about these questions. If you're studying alone, write down 2-3 sentences for each question. There is no correct answer—give your opinion or share your ideas

1. How do people celebrate Halloween in your country?
2. Have you ever dressed up for Halloween or gone trick-or-treating? How was it?
3. What's your favourite holiday to celebrate? Why?
4. Do you know the history behind Halloween? Look it up on the Internet if you don't.

Taking the Ferry

Reading strategy focus: *Look at the words in **bold**. If you don't know the meaning, make a guess based on the other words in the sentence. Do not use a dictionary. Then, read the questions below and the story.*

Min-Gyu and Ho-Hyun are two expats living in Victoria, studying at the University of Victoria. It is a beautiful old city on Vancouver Island but it's kind of boring. Lots of **seniors** move to Victoria from other parts of Canada when they **retire** because it's not as cold there. Plus, there are lots of other older people there to be friends with!

For **spring break**, the two friends decided to go to Vancouver, about a 3-hour ferry ride from Victoria. Min-Gyu said that they could take his car. You can also fly between the two cities but they decided that it'd be more convenient to have their own car because they could go to Whistler and have more freedom to go wherever else they wanted to go. It would be cheaper to just take the ferry instead of flying, and they were broke students.

Ho-Hyun did some research and booked a cheap **hostel** for them to stay in. He also looked on websites like *Trip Advisor* and wrote down some of the places that he wanted to visit, like Stanley Park and Capilano Canyon. Plus, he found some restaurants to try. Min-Gyu said he'd love to visit "Little Korea" on Robson Street downtown. They have Korean karaoke, Korean restaurants, and other things like that.

Ho-hyun looked on the BC Ferry website and suggested that they take the 9:35 am ferry. They were going to leave campus at 7:30 in order to get there on time.

The day of the trip arrived, and Min-Gyu was a little bit late! He loved to sleep in usually and getting up at 6:30 was early for him. They arrived at the ferry terminal at 8:45, **shocked** to see huge line-ups. They had to wait more than 30 minutes, even to talk to a **ticket agent**. When they finally talked to him, it was bad news! The 9:35 ferry was full already. And the 11:30 one as well. Everyone was going somewhere for spring break. They'd have to wait for the 1:45 ferry. They reluctantly agreed and bought the ticket. They had no other choice. Eventually, they made it to Vancouver and had a great time. And, they made a ferry reservation for the return trip! They didn't want to have to wait so long on the way home.

Vocabulary

spring break: Vacation from school, usually in February, March or April.

seniors: People over the age of 65.

retire: Stop working, usually at a certain age.

hostel: A cheaper version of a hotel. Usually with shared rooms.

shocked: Surprised.

ticket agent: Person who sells tickets.

Comprehension Questions

1. What's Victoria like?
2. Why do people retire in Victoria?
3. How are the two friends going to get to Vancouver?
4. Was the ferry terminal busy?
5. Did they catch the 9:35 ferry?
6. What did they do for the return trip?

Answers

1. It's beautiful but a little bit boring. There are lots of seniors there.
2. They retire there because the weather is not as cold as the rest of Canada.
3. They are going to drive and take the ferry.
4. Yes, it was busy because of spring break.
5. No, it was full. So was the next one. They'd have to take the third ferry.
6. They made a ferry reservation.

Synonym Practice: Think of two other words or phrases that have the same meaning as the vocabulary words from the story. Do NOT look at the definitions again, if possible.

1. seniors: _____, _____

2. shocked: _____, _____

3. hostel: _____, _____

Summarize the Story

Using 1-2 sentences, summarize the story. Include only the main details and key events.

Summary:

New Words

Write down any new words that you learned from this story. Consider writing them in a vocabulary notebook or making some flashcards for further review.

-

-

-

Let's Talk More

Talk with a friend or classmate about these questions. If you're studying alone, write down 2-3 sentences for each question. There is no correct answer—give your opinion or share your ideas!

1. Have you ever had to wait in line a long time because you didn't make a reservation?
2. Do people take ferries anywhere in your city? Where do they go?
3. Have you ever stayed in a hostel when travelling? How was your experience?
4. The two friends thought that Victoria was beautiful but kind of boring. How would you describe the city you live in?
5. Are you a night owl? A morning person? Neither?

Going Vegan

Reading strategy focus: *Scan the story quickly (set a timer for 30 seconds). Answer this question: Does Tony eat healthy food these days? (yes/no). See answer below the story. Then, read the questions and read the story again, more slowly.*

Tony was bored one night and was hanging out on his couch, eating potato chips and watching *Netflix*. He was supposed to **work out** with his friend, but he cancelled at the last minute. He was way too lazy to go exercise by himself, so he settled for sitting on the couch. He hated going to the gym alone and would only go if his friend encouraged him.

He didn't have a show that he was watching, so he was just **flipping around** randomly. He thought to himself that he should watch a documentary so that he could learn something! He found one that had an interesting title, "Forks over Knives." He started watching and found it quite good, despite not being the kind of thing that he usually watched. He usually loved watching things like action movies.

The **gist** of it was that eating less meat and animal products and more things like vegetables can make you healthier. You'll have fewer heart attacks and strokes and are also less likely to get cancer. Tony started to feel a little bit uncomfortable and put the potato chips back in the cupboard and got a glass of water. His doctor had recently told him that his **cholesterol** was too high and to start eating more fruits and vegetables and less meat.

He kept watching. By the end, he was convinced that he needed to change his diet and stop eating so much meat. If he kept living like he was now, he thought he'd die early for sure. It wouldn't be easy, but he was convinced that it was important.

Tony got out his computer and did lots of research and found some **vegan** and **plant-based** people on *Instagram* that had some delicious looking recipes. He ordered a couple of vegan cookbooks online: *Oh She Glows* and *Thug Kitchen*. Both of them had excellent reviews. He even looked up some recipes online and made a list of things to buy at the grocery store so that he could start cooking healthier meals. And he even sent a text to his vegan coworker Liz, asking for her help. She was excited for him and said that she'd love to help him out with it. He also decided to try eating vegan for one month and then get his cholesterol checked again to see what the effect was. He guessed that it would be much better.

Reading strategy focus answer: No, he doesn't.

Vocabulary

work out: Exercise.

flipping around: Using a remote control to scroll through TV or radio channels quickly.

gist: Short summary.

cholesterol: A fatty substance found in the blood and cells. Too much is bad for your health. It generally comes from eating animal products.

vegan: People who don't eat animal products, including things like milk, honey, eggs, etc.

plant-based: Similar to vegan but refers to eating mostly things that grow, as opposed to things that come from animals.

Comprehension Questions

1. Why was Tony sitting on the couch watching *Netflix*?
2. Why did he want to watch a documentary?
3. Why did he choose *Forks Over Knives*?
4. Did he believe what he saw in that documentary?
5. Why did he decide to make a change in his diet?
6. What steps did he take to go more plant-based?

Answers

1. He was sitting on the couch watching *Netflix* because his friend cancelled their plan, and he didn't want to go by himself.
2. He was hoping to learn something.
3. He chose it because he wanted to learn something, and it caught his attention.
4. Yes, he was convinced that he needed to stop eating so many animal products.
5. He decided to make a change because he thought he'd die early if he didn't.

6. He followed some people on *Instagram*, bought some cookbooks, found some recipes, made a shopping list, and texted his vegan coworker.

Synonym Practice: Think of two other words or phrases that have the same meaning as the vocabulary words from the story. Do NOT look at the definitions again, if possible.

1. work out: _____, _____
2. plant based _____, _____
3. gist: _____, _____

Summarize the Story

Using 1-2 sentences, summarize the story. Include only the main details and key events.

Summary:

New Words

Write down any new words that you learned from this story. Consider writing them in a vocabulary notebook or making some flashcards for further review.

-

-

-

Let's Talk More

Talk with a friend or classmate about these questions. If you're studying alone, write down 2-3 sentences for each question. There is no correct answer—give your opinion!

1. Would you ever consider becoming a vegan?
2. Are you a generally healthy or unhealthy eater? Give some examples.
3. Are you becoming more worried about your health, the older you get?

Getting a Part-Time Job

Reading strategy focus: *Look at the words in **bold**. If you don't know the meaning, make a guess based on the other words in the sentence. Do not use a dictionary. Then, read the questions below and the story.*

Mike was a high-school student in Halifax, Nova Scotia. His parents gave him an **allowance** of $20/week which was more than many of his friends got. However, it wasn't enough to go out with his friends all the time to watch movies or hang out at the mall. Most of his friends have **part-time jobs,** so they had more money than he did. He was a little bit jealous of them being able to buy new clothes or snacks whenever they wanted.

Mike had lots of free time, so he talked to his parents about getting a part-time job. His mom said that as long as he still got A's and B's in his classes, it was fine. She also said that she'd give him a ride to work or he could borrow her car as long as it wasn't too far away from their house. The only problem was that Mike didn't have any work experience. But most of his friends didn't have any work experience either when they got their first jobs.

He talked to his friends at school about their part-time jobs. They gave him some advice like avoiding a certain restaurant where the boss was terrible, or to not do something like **landscaping** because it was too difficult working in the rain or even snow all day.

A few of his friends worked at McDonald's, so he decided to apply there. It would be fun to work with his friends. It wasn't far from his high school so he walked over after school one day, before taking the bus home. He saw a sign outside that said they were hiring. He went inside and asked the person working there for an **application form.** She pointed out where they were on the wall. He grabbed one and sat down in a **booth** to fill it out. It was quite simple and asked for basic information like his name and phone number and took only a few minutes to fill out.

When he was finished, he asked one of the employees if he could talk to a manager.

He gave her his application and she mentioned that they needed people right away and asked if he could do an interview then. He said that he had some time so they sat down in a booth and talked for a few minutes. She asked some easy questions about **customer service** and what he would do in certain situations like if someone was complaining about something. The manager thanked him and said she'd give him a call in a day or two. Hopefully he got the job!

Vocabulary

allowance: Money that parents give their children on a weekly or monthly basis.

part-time job: A job that is less than 40 hours/week.

landscaping: Making a yard (or other outside space) more attractive/orderly by cutting the grass, trimming bushes, etc.

application form: What you fill out if you want to get a job.

booth: In a restaurant, a table with benches on either side.

customer service: What employees provide people who buy or use a service at a company. In a fast food restaurant, it involves taking orders and money, serving food, etc.

Comprehension Questions

1. Why did Mike want to get a part-time job?
2. Were his parents supportive of him getting a job?
3. Did most of his friends have jobs?
4. Why did his friends think that landscaping wasn't a great job?
5. Was McDonald's hiring people?
6. Did Mike find it difficult to fill out the application form and do the interview?

Answers

1. He wanted to get a job because he wanted to have more spending money.
2. Yes, as long as he continued to get good grades in school.
3. Yes, they did.
4. They said it wasn't good because you had to work outside in bad weather.
5. Yes, they needed people right away.
6. No, both those things were quite easy.

Synonym Practice: Think of two other words or phrases that have the same meaning as the

vocabulary words from the story. Do NOT look at the definitions again, if possible.

1. allowance: _____, _____

2. part-time job _____, _____

Summarize the Story

Using 1-2 sentences, summarize the story. Include only the main details and key events.

Summary:

New Words

Write down any new words that you learned from this story. Consider writing them in a vocabulary notebook or making some flashcards for further review.

-

-

-

Let's Talk More

Talk with a friend or classmate about these questions. If you're studying alone, write down 2-3 sentences for each question. There is no correct answer—give your opinion or share your ideas!

1. Did you get an allowance when you were a kid? How much did you get? What did you have to do for it?

2. Did you have a part-time job in high school or university? What did you do?

3. Do you think high-school students should have jobs? Or, should they only study?

4. Is it difficult to get a job in your country if you don't have any work experience?

Before You Go

If you found this book useful, please leave a review wherever you bought it. It will help other English learners, like yourself find this resource.

Please send me an email with any questions or feedback that you might have.

YouTube: www.youtube.com/c/jackiebolen

Pinterest: www.pinterest.com/eslspeaking

ESL Speaking: www.eslspeaking.org

Email: jb.business.online@gmail.com

You might also be interested in these books (by Jackie Bolen):

* Master English Collocations in 15 Minutes a Day

* IELTS Academic Vocabulary Builder

Printed by Amazon Italia Logistica S.r.l.
Torrazza Piemonte (TO), Italy

53890558R00063